THE
{SUPER-DELUXE}
EPIC JOURNAL
OF AWESOMENESS

DOVER PUBLICATIONS, INC.
MINEOLA, NEW YORK

ARTWORK PROVIDED BY HOURGLASS PRESS
IN PARTNERSHIP WITH
CORAL COMMUNICATIONS & DESIGN

GRAPHIC DESIGN BY SAUL SAUZA

Bibliographical Note
The Super-Deluxe, Epic Journal of Awesomeness is a new work,
first published by Dover Publications, Inc., in 2015.

International Standard Book Number
ISBN-13: 978-0-486-78328-4
ISBN-10: 0-486-78328-6

Manufactured in the United States by RR Donnelley
78328602   2015
www.doverpublications.com

How many folds
CAN YOU MAKE OUT
OF THIS PAGE?

COUNT: _____

USE THREE COLORS
to draw your favorite fruits
on this stand

If you could have a

TATTOO

WHAT WOULD IT BE?

draw it here:

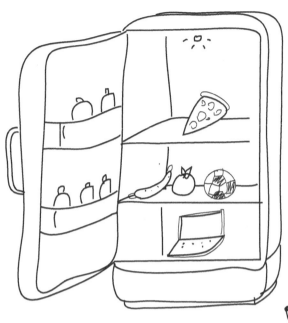

Draw the 5 most essential things you have in your FRIDGE

SKETCH 3 THINGS YOU LOST AND ARE SORRY YOU NEVER FOUND

Lost & Found

COLLECT YOUR FAVORITE CANDY HERE

WHAT'S INSIDE
YOUR STOMACH ?

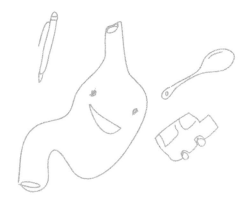

place you and your best friend
in a cartoon strip !

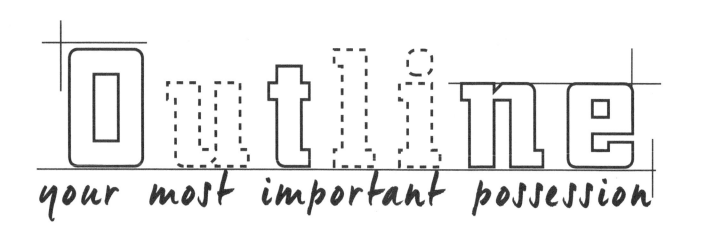

Outline
your most important possession

DRAW AND THEN COUNT ALL THE BUTTONS YOU ARE WEARING

ZIPPERS COUNT
AS DOUBLE

HOW MANY? : _____

DRAW ALL THE furniture IN YOUR ROOM on this page

CUT THIS SQUARE OUT

and fold it into an

ORIGAMI
CRANE

Turn over for instructions

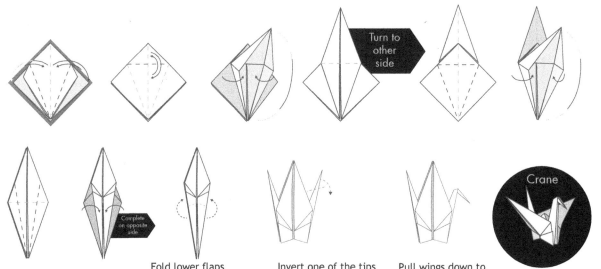

Fold lower flaps
upward, inverting them

Invert one of the tips
to create a head

Pull wings down to
complete the CRANE

Complete
on opposite
side

Turn to
other
side

Crane

PLACE A LEAF UNDERNEATH THIS PAGE, and with the flat side of a pencil, rub over the shape... recreate nature!

WAVE YOUR MAGIC WAND AND CHANGE THIS PIECE OF PAPER INTO CANDY.

DRAW WHAT IT LOOKS LIKE

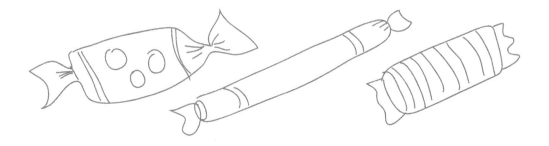

Find your favorite
painting and make your own
version of it with crayons

YOU ARE AN
ARCHITECT.

DRAW YOUR
DREAMHOUSE

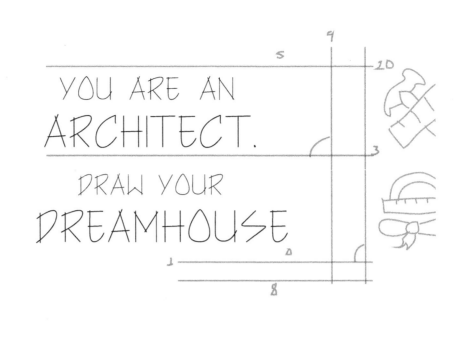

ILLUSTRATE YOUR FAVORITE SONG

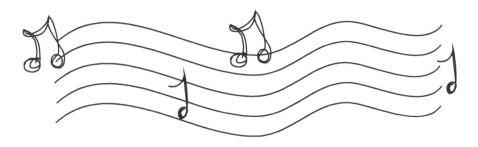

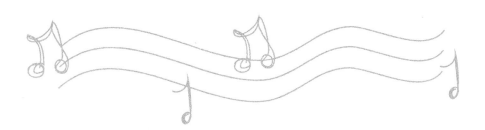

FIND THE DIFFERENCES
AND CIRCLE THEM.

HOW MANY DID YOU FIND?:

DRAW WHAT YOU WOULD LOOK LIKE IF YOU WERE A GIANT IN YOUR TOWN/CITY.

What's your favorite food in the morning?
show it below

DRAW YOUR FAVORITE
CANDY WRAPPER ON THIS PAGE

DRAW THE PLANET
YOU WOULD VISIT IF YOU HAD A
rocket ship

MAKE THIS A PALETTE
OF YOUR FAVORITE COLORS
for the Winter

MAKE THIS A PALETTE
OF YOUR FAVORITE COLORS
for the Spring

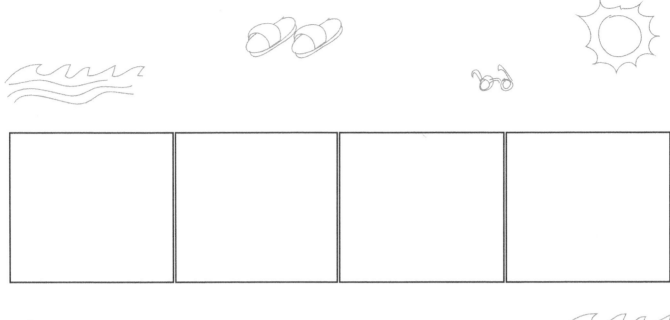

MAKE THIS A PALETTE
OF YOUR FAVORITE COLORS
for the Summer

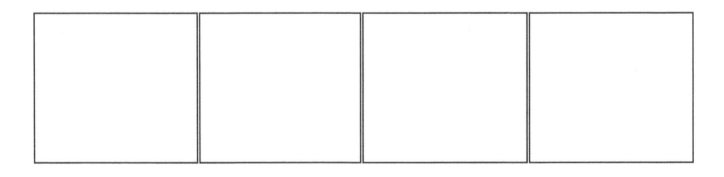

MAKE THIS A PALETTE
OF YOUR FAVORITE COLORS
for the Fall

Draw what's in your trash can today

Eat colored candy
and lick this page after

SHOW THE VIEW
FROM THE COCKPIT
OF YOUR AIRPLANE

DRAW your entire FAMILY as DOGS

Use this spread to fill in the menu of your future restaurant.

Fill your own name

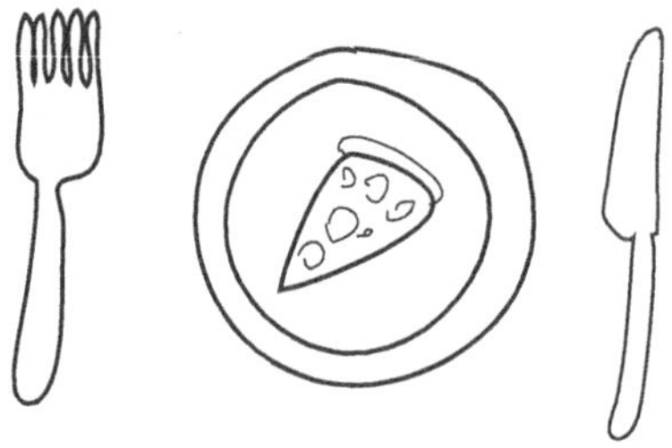

RESTAURANT

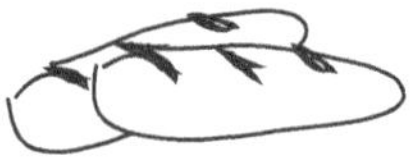

Breakfast

$

$

$

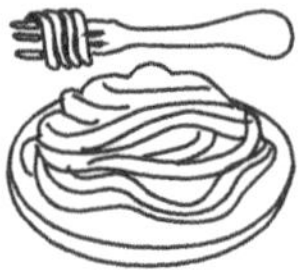

Pasta

$

$

$

Dinner

_____ $
_____ $
_____ $

Dessert

_____ $
_____ $
_____ $

Beverages

_____ $
_____ $
_____ $

SKETCH THE GARMENT
IN YOUR CLOSET THAT
YOU HAVE HAD FOR
THE LONGEST TIME.

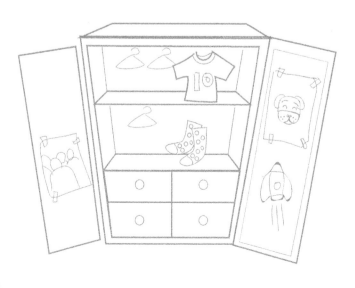

time's up

HOW many things
can you draw in 15 seconds?

4   5   1
5 3   4   6 0
6
4

THE DINOSAUR THAT REPRESENTS YOU MOST IS _____?

sketch it below

IF YOUR MIND WERE AN 8GB USB DRIVE, LIST ALL THE STUFF YOU WOULD LIKE TO SAVE ON IT.

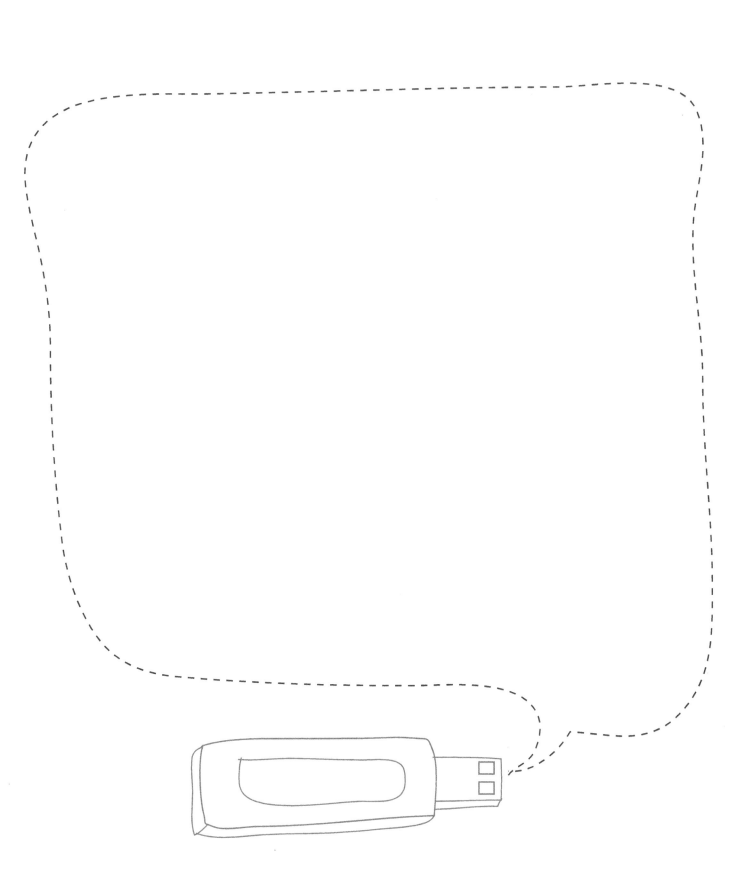

DRAW YOUR FAVORITE TOPPINGS ON YOUR PIZZA

Write the lyrics to your favorite song that you sing in the shower

Word fun

Use these words to create as many sentences as you can...

(you can make the words plural if you need to)

pencil

car   wishing

eight   moon

water

wish   hug

happy   pray

pink

closet

sock   board

ring

sun

black   to   has

purple

they

going   the

_____

_____

_____

_____

_____

_____

this   it   tomorrow   flower

mouse   of   by   the   to

father   Sunday   our

he   threw   found   water

_____

_____

_____

_____

_____

_____

_____

_____

_____

_____

_____

mind   being   if

be   glass   blue   those

she   brother   two

banana   mom   my

of

sister   yours   Friday

YOU ARE A BAKER.

DECORATE A BIRTHDAY CAKE

DRAW YOUR DAY AT THE BEACH

USE THIS SPREAD TO DRAW A MAP OF YOUR TOWN / CITY..

Use this legend to mark the places where...

I go once a month

* I go two - three times a month

! I go every two months

/ I go every three months

< I go every six months

● I go only if I have to go

? I never go

make a doodle
with your eyes closed ...

...What does it look like?

 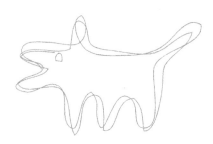 

Draw your face without taking your pen off the page

"IF YOU HAD A PET
FROM OUTER SPACE
DRAW IT BELOW"

You are a famous sports athlete.
Draw your uniform

Draw your pet shark

What does your town / city look like from a bird's-eye view?

DRAW YOUR UNDERSEA WORLD

WHAT DO THE MONSTERS UNDER YOUR BED LOOK LIKE ?

DRAW YOURSELF AS A SUPERHERO

LIFE COUPONS

Cut these and hand them out

ONE FREE HUG

TWO HUGS

One Back Rub
(non-refundable)

Clean up my room

LIFE COUPONS

CUT THESE AND HAND THEM OUT

ONE FREE HUG

TWO HUGS

One Back Rub (non-refundable)

Clean up my room

Draw your favorite
MODE OF TRANSPORTATION

WHERE DO YOU WANT TO GO? _____

WHAT DOES YOUR COMPUTER
SCREENSAVER LOOK LIKE?

SHOW YOUR FAVORITE
HOLIDAY GIFT,
WRAPPED AND UNWRAPPED